MYSTICAL EXPERIENCES IN 30 DAYS

MYSTICAL EXPERIENCES IN 30 DAYS

THE HIGHER CONSCIOUSNESS PROGRAM

KEITH HARARY, PH.D., AND PAMELA WEINTRAUB

ST. MARTIN'S PRESS
NEW YORK

Library of Congress Cataloging-in-Publication Data

Harary, Keith.
    Mystical experiences in 30 days : the higher consciousness program /
Keith Harary and Pamela Weintraub.
      p.   cm.
    ISBN 0-312-05133-6
    1. Altered states of consciousness. 2. Mysticism.
I. Weintraub, Pamela. II. Title.
III. Title: Mystical experiences in thirty days.
BF1045.A48H37   1990
131—dc20
                                                  90-37268
                                                  CIP

First Edition: September 1990

10 9 8 7 6 5 4 3 2 1

For Dr. George Kokoris,
who has always known that reality
is more than meets the I.
And for Dr. Harry Perlowitz,
master navigator of inner journeys and quests.

CONTENTS

INTRODUCTION

Most of us think of the mystical experience as a state of mind available only to those who meditate for years, live in some exotic culture, or take psychedelic drugs. The reality, however, is that mystical experiences are more commonplace than we think. They usually occur in fleeting, spontaneous moments, taking the form of a momentary shift in awareness, a sense of déjà vu, or a feeling of connectedness to something greater than the self. These experiences often occur during times of overwhelming emotional intensity, and are especially prevalent during profound interpersonal events like childbirth or falling in love.

In the Higher Consciousness Program, however, we will teach you to induce such experiences virtually at will. You will be able to do so, moreover, without taking drugs or dramatically altering your belief systems in any way. Your special tools: the Higher Consciousness Program exercises, which will teach you to pay attention to subtle feelings, ideas, and capabilities already present just beneath the superficial layers of everyday awareness. By shifting your awareness from mundane concerns, you can learn to experience life from the vantage point of the sage.

As you practice the exercises in the Higher Consciousness Program, you may feel at one with the universe. Your rigid concept of time should give way to a sense of timelessness, blurring the distinctions between past, present, and future. You will learn to evoke a sense of mystical reverie. And you may even feel a greater personal understanding of basic reality and everyday relationships and events.

Though the experiences induced by the Higher Consciousness Program exercises may be momentary in nature, they can have a profound and permanent impact on your life.

You should sense that impact almost at once. Starting with Week One, you will learn the technique of "perceptual focusing," in which you concentrate on minute details in the environment. As you develop the ability to focus your attention like a laser, you should eventually learn to transform your perception of any given object. For instance, you'll learn to focus on an object like a teacup until you can literally envision it on the molecular—and even the quantum—level. As a result, you should realize that you and the objects around you are made of the same basic stuff. And you should come to see reality in the form of a unified, continuous whole.

During Week Two, you will learn how to tap the mystical in everyday places and things. For instance, you will learn to have transcendent experiences by focusing on color and light. You will find the mystical in the constellations, the evening news, and the silence of night. You will also begin to induce *momentary* states of higher consciousness as a way of accessing your hidden capabilities and enhancing your relationship to friends, lovers, and society as a whole.

By the third week of the Higher Consciousness Program, you should be inducing a range of mystical experiences on an ongoing basis. You will, for instance, learn to share mystical experiences with a partner; to mentally "merge" with other life forms; and to induce mystical experiences through intimate contact and sex.

Finally, in Week Four you will study "spatial and temporal shifting," in which you consciously manipulate your perceptions of space and time. During this part of the program, for instance, you will "communicate" with your childhood self, tapping into dreams and goals that had long seemed lost, and with your future self, seeking advice from the person you believe you may become.

In our experience, the best way to induce mystical states is a step at a time. Give yourself time to focus on each of the Higher Consciousness Program exercises, and don't rush it. Although the program is designed to be carried out in 30 days, don't feel bound by this; it's perfectly acceptable to take longer to complete the program. So feel free to adapt our 30-day approach to suit your own needs and schedule.

We do not recommend completing the Higher Consciousness Program in less than 30 days, however, or trying to squeeze an entire week's worth of exercises into a single weekend. Although many of the Higher Consciousness Program exercises are conceptually quite simple, their combined impact could be profound. Ultimately you will experience deeper and more gratifying mystical states if your abilities evolve gradually, giving you the opportunity to adjust to your expanded perspective.

Please understand that mystical states may spontaneously emerge *at any point* in the Higher Consciousness Program. Indeed, Higher Consciousness is not a strictly linear process in which the goal is reached or not reached at the end of an exercise or series of exercises. Rather, this program is designed to interact, in an ongoing fashion, with each individual participant. It helps set the appropriate internal conditions for mystical experiences, it gets things moving, but the exact timetable for transcendence is up to *you*. This means that mystical states may be achieved easily and immediately by one individual, and much later, with far more difficulty, by another. Some of you may begin to have your first truly mystical experiences only after the 30-day period, when you have absorbed the program in full and integrated the information on a deep, inner level.

We want to emphasize that it would be most unusual for anyone to report problems as a result of the Higher Consciousness Program, especially since the program does not attempt to replace psychotherapy in any way, shape, or form. However, if you have a history of emotional or psychiatric problems, or if you feel at all uncomfortable about any of the exercises, we suggest you check with your therapist or psychiatrist before proceeding. In such a case, you might wish to carry out the Higher Consciousness Program only under his or her continued clinical guidance. Remember, you can terminate any exercise whenever you decide to do so; ending an exercise at one point will not diminish your ability to follow through with it more completely at a later time. In any event, we recommend that you practice the Higher Consciousness Program exercises only when you're sober, feeling emotionally relaxed and comfortable, and are unlikely to be interrupted by outside disturbances.

No matter who you are, the Higher Consciousness Program has been designed for your enjoyment. As you gain experience, you should be able to induce mystical states that are increasingly vivid and powerful. You should also find yourself exploring expansive internal realms and feeling ever more connected to your loved ones, the Earth, and the universe at large. In the end, mystical experiences should empower you, revealing hidden stores of energy and wisdom and a sense of wonder in life.

MYSTICAL
EXPERIENCES
IN 30 DAYS

**WEEK
ONE**

ONE STEP BEYOND

WEEK ONE

•

ONE STEP
BEYOND

What does it mean, as Ram Dass once suggested, to "be here now"? Where is "here," anyway, and what is "now"? Who, for that matter, are *you*?

Your answers to these questions depend entirely on your personal, *subjective*, perspective. And that perspective, in turn, is determined by your personal frame of reference—the way in which you have learned to observe the world.

If you learn to observe familiar things in new and different ways, your perception of everyday reality should broaden and change. In the process, you should move toward Higher Consciousness—a mystical perspective from which you may experience unexpected insights into the nature of reality and a sense of connectedness to the earth and the universe as a whole.

The first step in achieving Higher Consciousness is learning to pierce the veil of ordinary perception—and that is just what Week One of the Higher Consciousness Program will help you do. Your primary Week One tool? A technique known as "perceptual focusing," through which you can induce an altered state of consciousness by focusing on minute and particular details in your immediate environment. The resulting laserlike view should eventually transform your perception of objects and people. You should feel more in tune with yourself, the Earth, and the universe, and a sense of transcendence should begin to evolve within.

If there's a lesson to be learned during Week One, it is that you

p out of society, move to the Himalayas, or eat
years to develop a sense of Higher Consciousness.
learn as you practice the first seven exercises, the
contains all the elements needed to experience reality
inating ways.

DAY 1

THE YOU
NOBODY KNOWS

Who are you? A construction worker, teacher, bartender, or computer programmer? A parent, a child, or a lover to your spouse? Are you an American? A member of Mensa? A Vietnam veteran? Or do you conceive of yourself in even broader, more abstract terms: adventurer, dreamer, artist, activist, or survivor of life?

Now, who are you when you peel away these outer layers of identity and reach into the inner core of your personal existence? Does some deeper, more basic and immutable aspect of your identity—your "inner" self—lie waiting to be discovered beneath these everyday roles? In the following exercise, you will explore this possibility by pretending that all your memories are merely products of your imagination.

Begin by choosing a place where you can be completely alone for a couple of hours. (You may also practice this exercise if you're alone among a group of strangers—on an airplane, for example, or in a movie theater.) Sit in a comfortable position, close your eyes, and take a deep breath. As you continue to breathe in and out slowly, let your life pass before you: Recall childhood events, adolescent experiences, major life accomplishments or mistakes, memories of family members and friends. Don't become analytical about past relationships or get stuck on particular experiences. Just let your impressions come and go. How does it feel to be the person you've become?

After you've allowed yourself to focus on these thoughts for at least half an hour, take another deep breath. As you breathe, concentrate on how alone you are at this moment. Pay attention to your physical environment and your body's sensations. Continue to breathe slowly.

Now envision the experiences you have just recalled fading in a mist. Imagine that your present situation and immediate surroundings represent the whole of reality. Everything you remembered about the world and your life, the people and events in it, is imaginary. In fact, you've just come into existence in the past few moments. Continue to focus your imagination on this idea for at least another hour and a half.

Now ask yourself this: If everything you remember about your life is a product of your imagination, who are you? Is there some aspect of your existence—a particular set of values or a relationship with another person—that appears to transcend mundane levels of reality and that is impossible to imagine as an illusion?

In the last half hour of this exercise, allow yourself to imagine that you were born into a completely different life. Is there a "real you" that would still be there even if you had been born in another place and time, existed in a completely different reality, or weren't even human? What aspects of your personal identity—if any—would continue, unchanged, had you been born in the days of King Arthur, or had you lived as a giant octopus on the ocean floor?

Finally, take another deep breath. As you let it out, ask yourself how you know that your life, as you experience it, really exists at all. How do you know you are not merely imagining the details of your everyday existence? For all you know, you may really be a slime mold growing on some forgotten rock, so bored and miserable with life as you know it that you have simply imagined the details and complications of an apparent human existence as a distraction.

After you have entertained yourself with this bizarre concept for a while, allow your thoughts to drift back to the everyday world.

Transcendental Tip—With regular practice, this exercise can help you approach everyday reality in a different way: not as boring, habitual, or conflicted, but rather as a realm of expanded possibility that responds to your true creative self. This exercise can also put you in touch with the most sacred, enduring aspects of your life and help you to appreciate qualities that do not depend upon the transitory, material world.

DAY 2

THE PASSING
PARADE

On Day 2 you will focus on inducing a Mystical Experience by altering your perceptions of the people around you. Pick a crowded location full of strangers: a busy airport, train station, or shopping mall will do. Spend anywhere from two to four hours sitting in one place observing the people milling about.

Take time to observe your surroundings and experience the various sensory experiences that are available in the location you've chosen. Notice the stationary aspects of your environment—benches, vending machines, newsstands, restaurants, and coffeehouses. Then notice the things that are in a continuous state of change, such as the activities of the crowd and the coming and going of buses, trains, cars, or airplanes. After an hour you'll probably notice underlying patterns in the surrounding activity.

You may notice the broad patterns of moving objects or vehicles, and the far more subtle patterns of the crowd. You may also notice that the individuals moving in cars or on foot are unaware of their "patterned" roles. Behind the patterns of moving objects and people lie still broader patterns defined by society, the earth, and the universe. How are the lives of the people you're observing influenced by the sweeping patterns of which they may be unaware?

As you watch the people all around you, consider the possibility that no one else experiences reality exactly as you do. Pick out a stranger and, without disturbing this individual, compare your reality to his. Don't dwell on superficial differences such as physical appearance, racial identity, or cultural background. Instead, focus on the possibility that the world may be a unique and radically different experience for each of you. Your usually unstated assumption—"I share the same reality with this stranger"—may be only an illusion.

It is, in fact, logically impossible to prove for certain that any two individuals are perceiving exactly the same reality, because each of you would interpret those differences within your familiar frame of reference. Ask yourself, for example, if you have any way of knowing if you and the stranger you have chosen perceive the color red in exactly the same way.

Now relax, take a deep breath, and turn your attention back to your general surroundings. Instead of focusing on the possible uniqueness of your personal perceptions, consider what you have in common with the people you're watching. You're all alive at this particular moment in human history; your lives have crossed paths, even if at a comfortable distance. Even if you never speak to one another and are never again in the same place, there will always be a time in your mutual past when your paths crossed. If the world or your life were to end at this moment, it would end for you in the company of these strangers.

But you do not have to face death to sense such camaraderie. Instead, just imagine that a part of you can perceive reality from the perspective of ''the group mind.'' For this portion of the exercise, picture yourself and the strangers you're watching as a single group, one organic entity moving without individual perceptions. Envision the environment you are sharing as a single, finely tuned organism, and see yourself and others as individual cells. Allow yourself to feel as connected as possible to those around you, and note the ways in which you are all bound together through your membership in the greater whole.

Now, once more, consider the notion that reality is subjective—that the world as you know it is exclusively manufactured within the innermost recesses of your mind. Ask yourself: ''If I am alone in the way I perceive reality, what do my perceptions tell me about who I am?'' Repeat this question to yourself until its deeper meaning sinks in.

Finally, spend half an hour or so exploring your local surroundings on foot. Continue to imagine that your experience of reality is entirely subjective. Study the people and objects all around you, and imagine that everything you see exists on at least two levels: the level at which you personally experience it, and the level at which it expresses its own objective nature. Then, taking this approach further, ask yourself: ''If there is an objective reality hidden behind the layers of everyday reality as I experience it, what might that deeper reality be like?'' Try to envision that other reality in as much detail as possible.

> **Transcendental Tip**—Now consider the fact that no matter how seriously you try to envision a deeper reality, you will inevitably interpret your experience through the subjective limitations of your own perceptions and intelligence.

Complete this exercise by celebrating the joys of mundane reality. Treat yourself to an ice cream sundae, go to a shopping mall, or feed the pigeons in a nearby park. Allow yourself to enjoy your unique subjective experience of the everyday world.

DAY 3

UNIFIED FIELDS

Mystics have long claimed that reality is unified—that if we could perceive the true nature of the universe, we would realize that everything is connected to everything else. Through today's exercise, you should be able to experience reality from this alternate, mystical perspective, ultimately perceiving the world around you as a unified whole rather than as a collection of separate and independent parts.

To begin, choose any ordinary location where you can practice this exercise without being disturbed—your favorite chair, for instance, a park bench, or the beach. Allow yourself time to settle into the location you've chosen and become relaxed.

When you feel comfortable, focus on some common object in your immediate environment: a candy dish, for instance, a seashell, or a leaf. Any object will do, as long as it is close enough for you to focus on it to the exclusion of everything else.

Take a deep breath and concentrate on the object until it's all you see or think about. (Even the most ordinary and familiar object can take on a surrealistic quality if you concentrate all your attention on it for an extended period of time.)

As you continue to focus, consider the physical structure of the object you have chosen. First notice its shape. Then, if it has more than one piece, notice how different parts are attached: with glue, for instance, or with nails. Now envision the object on a microscopic level: If it's a plant, see the individual cells. If it's a wood carving, see the individual grains of wood. Finally, consider the object on a molecular and quantum level: Envision the electrons whirling around the nuclei of the atoms, and tell yourself that both you and the object are made of the same basic types of particles. The particles constituting you and the object may even be bound together by physical fields. In other words, the sense that you are separate from other people and the rest of your environment may be a product of your perceptual limitations. It may have nothing to do with the way things are put together at all.

DAY 4

TRANSCENDING
TACK

In the art of Zen meditation, one can learn to focus so intensely upon the everyday world that the act of focusing, in and of itself, creates its own special sense of transcendence. On Day 4 of the Higher Consciousness Program, you'll begin exploring this type of experience for yourself by focusing on some of the more bizarre aspects of the world in which we live.

Begin today's exercise by visiting your local anthropology or natural history museum. If you absolutely cannot get to such a museum, you may substitute the anthropology section of your local bookstore or library. Your goal: to visit three separate exhibits representing three distinctly different human cultures. (Alternatively, you may review the artifacts of three cultures by flipping through photographs in various books.) As you explore the objects, don't allow yourself to become overly analytical. Instead, just spend your time absorbing the overall experience.

If you are visiting New York's American Museum of Natural

History, for example, you might begin by investigating the hall of Northwest Coast Indians and examining the giant totem poles, carved rattles, dyed blankets, and colorful masks. You might then proceed to the Central America exhibit, where you will encounter an Aztec sun wheel, stone fertility figures, and artifacts of gold. Then you might take the elevator to the hall of Man in Africa to study the skin drums and shrunken heads.

As you encounter the various objects, imagine what everyday reality must have been like for those who created them. How do your feelings toward reality shift as you move from exhibit to exhibit? How do these feelings differ from your usual feelings toward every-day reality?

For the second phase of this exercise, return home and choose some synthetically produced object that could have been manufac-tured only in contemporary society. Although many people mistak-enly believe that transcendent experiences can only be achieved through meditating for years on so-called sacred objects, this is not the case. By focusing on something ordinary, like a can of sardines or a baseball card, you can learn to appreciate transcendent levels of reality in the here and now.

The object you choose for this phase of the exercise should be as unredeemably tacky as possible. It should ideally (though not necessarily) represent something in the ''natural'' world, yet not be natural at all. A plastic Halloween mask of Bugs Bunny, Daffy Duck, or some other cartoon character would be ideal for this portion of the exercise, as would a bunch of plastic flowers, a rubber hand, a piece of wax fruit, or a toy stuffed animal with fluorescent fur.

Sit in a comfortable position with the object you have selected directly in front of you. Take a deep breath, feel all the muscles in your body letting go of any residual tension, and allow yourself to relax. Then close your eyes for a few minutes and calmly reflect upon your remembered mental images of the objects you encountered in the museum earlier in the day. Remember how those objects made you feel about the worldviews of those who created them. Then allow the memory of these ancient objects to fade.

Now, without otherwise moving your body, open your eyes and begin focusing exclusively on the contemporary object before you. Then imagine that you are an anthropologist from another culture— perhaps even another world—studying this object for the first time.

How does this object make you feel about the overall worldview of the culture that created it? Notice how these feelings differ from those you had earlier in the day, while you were examining objects from the past.

After you have maintained this focus for at least 10 to 15 minutes, gradually let go of any intellectual reflections about the object in question. Instead, focus on its independent existence as a thing in the universe. Note that the object exists apart from human values, history, or culture. Intensify your focus until all preconceived ideas about the object dissolve, and you feel as though you are appreciating its unique existence for the very first time.

You should be able to recognize when you have achieved this intense focus, because the object will cease to appear tacky and mass-produced. In fact, it won't appear to have any particular human value or function at all. Instead, it will seem to reflect an almost transcendent dimension of reality, placing you in touch with an ineffable inner truth. You should then feel as though you have finally recognized the object for exactly what it is—in and of itself—for the very first time.

Once you achieve a sense of transcendence, again allow yourself to experience the object as a somewhat surrealistic reflection of the day-to-day reality in which you live.

DAY 5

FANTASTIC
VOYAGE

In today's exercise, you will turn your attention toward your own body. Find a private and comfortable place where you can sit completely naked, and totally alone, for at least an hour. Position yourself on the floor in front of a mirror in a dimly lit room. The mirror should be positioned so that you may easily see your entire body without shifting from your initial position.

Keep your eyes open and focus your attention exclusively on

your reflection. Take a deep breath and, as you let it out, imagine warm currents of energy moving up through the soles of your feet, into your legs and hips, and gently relaxing your lower extremities. With your eyes still open, take another deep breath and, as you let it out, imagine the currents moving up through your abdomen and lower back, into your chest and arms, and relaxing your entire mid-section. Finally, take another deep breath and, as you let it out, imagine the currents moving up through your shoulders and neck, and out through the top of your head. It is not necessary to become completely relaxed for this exercise—only to let go of at least *some* tension, leaving stress from the outside world behind.

As soon as you begin to feel relaxed, look at your overall image in the mirror and say to yourself, in your thoughts, ''This is the surface of my body.'' Notice the surface of your skin, your body's general shape and overall form. Also note any especially distinctive characteristics, such as beauty marks, scars, and the general structure of your face. Then look into the reflection of your eyes and say to yourself, ''This is where I enter my body from the outside world.''

As you hear these words, imagine your conscious awareness shrinking down to the size of the period at the end of this sentence. Then imagine yourself floating into the reflected image of your own open eyes, and observing the hidden reality within your body.

Imagine your perceptions gradually turning more and more deeply inward, as though you were passing through layers of flesh, bones, and blood to begin exploring the complex microscopic universe within your physical form. As you probe more and more deeply, envision not only your underlying muscles, bones, blood vessels, and organs, but also the individual cells that make up the various parts of your body. Notice the organized and pulsating flow and rhythm of this inner universe, and imagine that you can hear your heart beating loudly in the background, your blood flowing through veins and arteries, and your lungs pumping in air from the outside world.

Then imagine your perceptions shrinking down to an even more primary level, until you are so small that your inner environment ceases to appear as a separate reality and instead becomes a universe of patterns and particles that merges and interacts with all the other patterns and particles in the universe at large.

Once you have achieved this focus and maintained it for a brief time, envision yourself growing larger once more. Again see yourself as a particle floating within a recognizable human body. Then turn your attention back toward the outside world and imagine yourself peering out of your body through your reflected eyes. Finally, shift your focus back to the here and now, and observe your body sitting across from the mirror on the floor.

As you look at your reflection, consider the ways in which your distinct and independent identity relies upon highly limited levels of perception and experience. How many levels of reality can you traverse and still be identifiably "you"?

DAY 6

GLOBAL REALITY

On Day 6, you will continue to practice the perceptual focusing technique you have learned this week. Instead of looking inward, however, you will turn your attention toward the outer world. Begin today's exercise by going for an hour-long walk in some more or less unspoiled setting not far from where you live. You may visit a park or beach, for example, where nature seems relatively untouched by the civilized world.

As you look around this natural spot, consider what the outlying environment might have been like had it never been overrun by civilization. What was the terrain of your city or town like before there were any roads or buildings? What animals did it contain? After you consider these questions, notice any plants, insects, birds, or animals in the natural spot you have chosen. Are there obvious ways in which they appear to be adapting to the encroachment of the civilization nearby?

As you continue your walk, eventually turn back toward a more developed area. Pay special attention to those aspects of your environment that continue to reflect the primal influence of nature despite the encroachment of civilization. For instance, do spiders spin their webs in the crevices of a building? Do grass or weeds grow up through tiny cracks in the sidewalk?

Find a spot where the edge of nature meets the edge of the civilized world. A bench on the outer perimeter of a large public park in the middle of a sprawling city would be an ideal spot to practice this exercise. So would a scenic overlook from which you can see a city skyline across some sizable body of water, a group of cabins at the edge of a national park, or a rooftop garden on top of an office building in your city's downtown area.

Now sit down, get comfortable, and spend about 20 minutes quietly observing the events taking place in both the natural and civilized portions of your world. Notice, especially, how you participate in both the civilized and natural realm by virtue of your simple presence.

> **Transcendental Tip**—As you follow through with this portion of the exercise, we would like you to notice how the civilized and natural worlds balance each other, forming the yin and yang of a single, organic reality. Also please note that human beings, themselves biological organisms, are also creations of nature. Since this is the case, then anything created by humans must have been created by nature as well. In other words, a skyscraper at the edge of Manhattan's Central Park is no less a natural creation than an anthill at the edge of the Serengeti.

To complete this exercise, imagine that the entire Earth, including the civilized and natural realms, constitutes a single living, breathing organism. Imagine that you are a cell floating within that greater organism, traversing back and forth between its component parts and participating in the process of nature, including every aspect of the civilized world as we know it today.

> **Transcendental Tip**—After you've completed this exercise, you may wish to consider the possibility that the Earth itself is just a single cell within the larger biological organism of the universe. As a single molecule within such a cell, you would also personally participate in even the most complex and unfathomable aspects of the universe as a whole.

DAY 7

A FRUITFUL
ENDEAVOR

Today you will celebrate everyday reality. To do so, select a piece of fruit with an easily removable peel—a banana, grapefruit, tangerine, or orange. Sit alone in a completely private place with the fruit you have selected and very slowly remove the peel. As you do so, take time to appreciate the fruit on as many sensory levels as possible. Smell the inside of the peel. Listen to the sound of the peel being pulled away from the inner fruit. Feel the texture and wetness of both the peel and the inside of the fruit. Observe the delicate inner structure and natural engineering of your particular piece of fruit. Then, finally, indulge yourself: Taste your fruit's recognizable flavor on the surface of your tongue.

As you eat, allow yourself to appreciate the fact that in the entire history of the universe, you are the only living creature who will ever know and experience the inside of this exact, virgin piece of fruit. A great many people have handled this piece of fruit during its growing and picking, during its shipping, and during its sale, but you are the only one to have known this piece of fruit in an intimate and personal way.

> *Transcendental Tip*—After you have practiced this consuming exercise, take the rest of the day off and balance your inner thoughts with unstructured physical activity, such as walking, working out at a gym, or playing tennis.

Congratulations! You've just completed Week One of the Higher Consciousness Program!

WEEK ONE   ONE STEP BEYOND

DAY 1 THE YOU NOBODY KNOWS		DAY 2 THE PASSING PARADE	
Choose a place where you can be alone or sit among a group of strangers. Close your eyes and relax.	Imagine that you were born into a different life. Once more ask yourself who you really are.	Spend two to four hours sitting in one place observing people in a crowded location full of strangers.	Envision your environment as one organism. Notice your participation in the greater whole.
Let your life pass before you. Focus on significant events and people.	Allow your thoughts to drift back to the everyday world.	Notice underlying patterns in the surrounding activity.	Ask yourself what your perceptions of reality tell you about who you are. Repeat this question to yourself until its deeper meaning sinks in.
After half an hour, concentrate on how alone you are at this moment. Pay attention to your environment and physical sensations.		Go over your own worldview. Ask yourself if you share that worldview with a nearby stranger.	Explore your surroundings on foot. Ask yourself if there is an objective reality other than the one you experience. Envision that other reality.
Imagine that your present situation and surroundings represent the whole of reality and that you've just come into existence. Ask yourself who you really are.		Consider what you have in common with the people you're watching.

Imagine that part of you can perceive reality from the perspective of "the group mind." | Celebrate mundane reality and your unique experience of the everyday world. |

DAY 3 UNIFIED FIELDS	**DAY 4** TRANSCENDING TACK		
Choose a place where you won't be disturbed. Settle in and relax.

Focus on an ordinary object to the exclusion of everything else.

Consider the surface structure of the object. Then envision the object on a microscopic level and on molecular and quantum levels.

Consider the deeper physical connections between you and the object. | Visit an anthropology or natural history museum or the anthropology section of a library or bookstore. Study artifacts from three different cultures.

Imagine what everyday reality must have been like for those who created the artifacts. Notice ways in which your feelings toward reality shift as you move from exhibit to exhibit or study photographs of objects from different cultures. | Return home. Choose a synthetically produced contemporary object that is as tacky as possible.

Sit with the object in front of you. Relax, close your eyes, and remember your experience of the objects you encountered earlier. Then allow the memory of those ancient objects to fade.

Open your eyes and focus on the contemporary object before you. Imagine that you are an anthropologist from another culture or world studying this object. | How does the object make you feel about the culture that created it? How do these feelings differ from those you had while you were examining objects from the past?

After 10 to 15 minutes, let go of any intellectual reflections about the object. Focus on its independent existence apart from human values, history, or culture. Allow your preconceived ideas about the object to dissolve, and appreciate its unique existence.

Allow your viewpoint to shift back to a more mundane perspective. |

DAY 5
FANTASTIC
VOYAGE

Find a private place where you can sit completely naked, and totally alone, for at least an hour.

Position yourself on the floor in front of a mirror in a dimly lit room. Keep your eyes open and focus on your reflection.

Enter a relaxed, yet alert state.

Focus on your image in the mirror. Imagine your awareness shrinking down and floating into the reflected image of your own open eyes. Observe the hidden reality within your body. Imagine your perceptions shrinking down even further, until your inner environment becomes a whirl of patterns and particles that merges with all the other patterns and particles in the universe.

Envision yourself growing larger. Again see yourself as a particle floating within your recognizable human body. Turn your attention back toward the outside world and imagine yourself peering out of your body through your reflected eyes.

Shift your focus back to the here and now and observe your body sitting across from the mirror on the floor.

Consider the ways in which your sense of personal identity relies upon limited levels of perception.

DAY 6
GLOBAL
REALITY

Go for an hour-long walk in an unspoiled setting not far from where you live.

Imagine what the environment might have been like had it never been overrun by civilization.

Eventually turn back toward a more developed area. Pay attention to those aspects of your environment that continue to reflect nature.

DAY 7
A FRUITFUL
ENDEAVOR

Find a spot where the edge of nature meets the edge of civilization. Spend 20 minutes observing events in both the natural and civilized aspects of your world. Notice your participation in both the civilized and natural realms.	Select a piece of fruit with an easily removable peel. Sit alone in a private place with the fruit you have selected and slowly remove the peel.
Imagine that the entire Earth constitutes a single organism. Focus on civilization as one aspect of nature and on your own participation in all aspects of the natural world.	Take time to appreciate the fruit on as many sensory levels as possible.
	Consider your intimate and personal knowledge of this unique piece of fruit.
	Take the rest of the day off and enjoy some unstructured physical activity.

WEEK
TWO

THE EVERYDAY MYSTIC

WEEK TWO

•

THE EVERYDAY MYSTIC

*D*uring Week Two of the Higher Consciousness Program, you will start integrating mystical experiences into your everyday life. Toward this end, you will learn to perceive the mystical in virtually all you encounter— light and color, the sounds of silence, the evening news, and the stars. In fact, by focusing on aspects of the world that you normally take for granted, mystical states of consciousness can become almost commonplace in your life.

As you continue to practice Week Two exercises, you should find yourself inducing mystical states of consciousness from moment to moment through the course of the day. And these *moments* of Higher Consciousness may ultimately have more impact on your sense of reality than similar states achieved by meditating for months or years or totally removing yourself from the world.

The reason is clear: When you distance yourself from the main-stream of life in order to achieve a ''higher'' state, you must, like it or not, eventually come down from the mountain and deal with the world. If you are unable to introduce a sense of awe and wonder into your experience of this world, you may wind up with no greater insight than you had before. Indeed, as mystics have claimed since time immemorial, being ''in this world but not of it''—achieving heightened awareness while continuing your ordinary life—may be the highest mystical state of all. After all, it's easy to focus on blissful detachment, cosmic consciousness, and nirvana while isolated in a desert cave. But if you can get beyond the spiritual, psychological, and social confinement of the real world *while still participating in it*, then you have truly achieved a mystical state of mind.

And as Week Two exercises will reveal, our everyday world has plenty of mystical stuff in store. Check out the light coming through your fire escape—it is no less mystical than the light falling on some distant temple. Check out the evening news. Its lessons are no less mystical than those of the Talmud. The colors of your polyester pajamas can be as transcendent as those of a holy monk's robes. The mood of night may be just as expansive from your apartment or a secluded Zen monastery. And the stars are equally inspiring when viewed from the parking deck at the local shopping mall or a cliff at the edge of the world.

Remember, as you explore the ordinary/extraordinary phenomena of your life in Week Two, to value subtle and delicate changes in perception as well as more expansive and exhilarating altered states. During Week Two you may experience both. But your primary goal will be learning to think like an everyday mystic. For once you have learned to glean the cosmic from the commonplace, you will begin to perceive mystical dimensions in every part of your life.

DAY 8

BROADCAST NEWS

Today you will tune in to the media and the way in which it has influenced your view of reality. Begin late this evening by turning off all the lights and turning on the 11:00 P.M. television news. We recommend the late news because the day's activities should be winding down and the bustle and noise should begin to subside. (If it's impossible for you to stay awake for the 11:00 P.M. news, you may substitute an earlier news broadcast.)

Leave the sound turned off and, focusing clearly on the picture, sit as far as possible from the screen. Now watch the facial expressions of the television news anchors as they introduce image after image and story after story. Do their facial expressions seem appropriate to the images they're presenting? Do they smile while introducing the news, then immediately reveal images of violence or tragedy? How much of the news is upbeat, and how much is downbeat? Pay particular attention to the way in which commercials are interspersed between the various reports.

As you sit in the dark watching these silent images, ask yourself how they affect your view of yourself, human nature, and the world. Imagine that you are a visitor from another world observing overall themes and patterns in human behavior for the first time. What can you learn?

After you have watched silent news images for 30 minutes, go about your business as usual, eventually retiring for sleep. Spend the rest of this week deliberately avoiding contact with television news, weekly news magazines, or newspapers. After a few days pass, you may begin to feel strangely disconnected from events in the world around you. By the end of the week, you should feel an odd sense of distance from global concerns.

Transcendental Tip—Unless World War III breaks out while you're looking the other way, you probably won't miss much you can't catch up with next week. Remember, you will continue to avoid the news until Day 14 of the Higher Consciousness Program.

Transcendental Tip—Before you fall asleep, be sure you read ahead to the exercise for Day 10 so that you will be able to start as soon as you wake up in the morning.

DAY 9

THE LIGHT
FANTASTIC

Sometimes the most fundamental aspects of reality can take on a transcendental dimension. Light, for instance, is a vital aspect of your everyday existence, yet, if you focus on it intensely, you can mentally transport yourself to different realms.

Begin this exercise first thing in the morning, before you even open your eyes. As you slowly come to consciousness, notice the way in which surrounding light filters through the surface of your eyelids. Then, slowly open your eyes and notice the various layers of light and shadow in the room around you.

Pay attention, for example, to any obvious lines of natural light that may be filtering in through your window. Notice, also, additional sources of light coming into your bedroom from surrounding rooms. Are there any spots in your room that are obviously brighter than adjacent spots? Are there lighted numbers on an electric clock radio, a TV, a CD player, or other appliances? Is any light from outside your room reflected in a mirror or some other smooth and shiny surface? Are there any especially dim or dark parts of your room where the light doesn't seem to reach at all?

Now switch on the room light. Notice how your perceptions—and even your sense of reality—shift the instant you throw the switch. You may, for example, feel as though you have suddenly and completely left the remembered world of last night to enter the immediate reality of today.

As you go about the rest of your day, pay special attention to your ongoing and almost unconscious interaction with light. As you enter any dark or dimly lit room, for example, notice how your feelings change as soon as you turn on the lights. Notice subtle differences in the way you may feel toward a room when it is lit by natural light, by incandescent light, or by fluorescent bulbs.

As you walk around outside during the course of your day, notice natural patterns of brightness and shadow at every level of your environment. Notice how plants and trees turn their vines and leaves toward the light. Notice that puddles glisten in the sun and observe how shadows dance on the pavement when wind blows the trees.

At sunset, stand outdoors or peer through your window and notice how your feelings subtly shift as light gives way to darkness. Then, after the sun has set, go for a walk and observe the way your sense of reality shifts with the darkness of night.

Notice the difference between the way your surroundings look after dark and the way these same surroundings appeared earlier in the day. Notice the stationary patterns of light created by streetlamps, and the shifting or moving patterns of light created by such things as flashing neon signs and passing cars.

Complete this exercise by sitting in an otherwise completely dark room with a burning candle a few feet away. Watch the flickering flame and notice the moving patterns of light and shadow it creates in the room around you. Then blow out the candle and sit in the dark for at least 20 minutes before turning on the lights.

As you focus on the all-pervasive, ever-shifting nature of light, you may become more fully conscious of the continuously shifting mental currents that define your relationship with everyday reality.

> ***Transcendental Tip***—Once you've spent an entire day practicing this exercise, you may also induce momentary higher consciousness states by focusing on patterns of light and shadows in your immediate environment for much briefer periods of time. You may, for example, practice this technique while sitting in the park or looking out the window during your lunch break. By tuning in to the subtleties of light, you can momentarily let go of the immediate pressures in your life. As you do so, you should feel more connected to the Earth and the universe around you.

DAY 10

COLOR
MY WORLD

On Day 10 you will focus on the role of color in your life. Begin by noticing the colors you choose to wear when you first get dressed in the morning. What mood do those colors communicate? How do they look against the colors of your skin, eyes, and hair? Notice the colors you've used to decorate your home. What color are your chairs and sofa, your bedspread, even your bathroom fixtures, towels, and plates?

As you leave your home for the day, notice the color of the sky, the buildings, the sidewalks, and the vegetation, including the hues of flowers and trees. Notice the colors adorning the animals, birds, and people you pass in the street. Then, as much as possible throughout the course of your day, focus on any objects you encounter not as objects in and of themselves, but rather as individual patches of color forming broader patterns of color in the world.

As you walk down the street, for example, notice the constantly changing colors of traffic lights; also notice the streaming patterns of color created by cars as they move in response to those lights. Focus on the colors of your work environment and the ways in which those colors both reflect and influence your feelings toward your job.

Sometime during the afternoon of Day 10, choose a particular color and focus exclusively on its presence in your life. If you choose the color red, for example, pay special attention to how often you encounter various shades and intensities of red in the course of your usual activities. If you have the time and inclination, you may then switch your focus to another color.

> ***Transcendental Tip***—In our experience, this simple exercise can have a profound impact on your level of awareness and your sense of self. Redefining your relationship to color can help you see the world—and your personal existence—in a new, more finely tuned light.

DAY 11

NIGHTHAWK

If you are in suitable physical and mental condition, and your doctor approves of this activity, you may be able to induce a sense of higher consciousness through deliberate sleep deprivation.

> ***Transcendental Tip***—Practice this exercise only when sleeplessness won't interfere with your livelihood or safety. Do not, for instance, drive a car or operate dangerous machinery without sleep. If you have any doubts about your physical or psychological ability to handle this exercise, simply proceed directly to Day 12.

Please conduct the following exercise at home or anyplace else where you will be completely safe and undisturbed for the entire night. Begin by vowing to remain awake for at least 24 hours. Tonight, tell yourself, you simply won't go to sleep at all.

To conserve your energy, don't engage in strenuous physical activity. Instead, use the time when you would normally be sleeping to pursue a quiet project that nonetheless requires concentration. You may write letters, cook, draw pictures, or build a model boat or plane. We suggest that you avoid just watching television, however, since passively viewing video images may actually lull you to sleep.

Transcendental Tip—As the hours pass, you may notice that time seems to pass in a slower, gentler way. Indeed, 8 hours in the social reality of your office in the middle of the day can seem to move at a much different pace than 8 hours spent doing something you enjoy at home alone in the middle of the night. Although an hour is exactly the same length of time in either event, your internal focus of attention has everything to do with how you'll experience it. This subjectively fluid dimension of time is something you can deliberately manipulate to create a variety of unusual states of mind.

As you begin to feel the effects of sleep deprivation, and as your sense of time shifts its boundaries, find a comfortable place to sit and look directly at an illuminated watch or clock that has a second hand sweeping around it. Dim the lights and then watch the clock for a while. Take a deep breath and think of a significant event to which you are really looking forward. Estimate the number of days before the event is scheduled to occur. Then estimate the number of hours, minutes, and seconds as well. Take another deep breath and watch the second hand sweep around the clock.

Transcendental Tip—By watching the clock, you will learn to manipulate your internal focus of attention and intentionally alter your perception of time.

Transcendental Tip—As you continue your sleep deprivation experience, you may find yourself slipping into various mystical states of mind without much deliberate effort. It is common in sleep deprivation, for example, to experience a sense of intense objectivity in which you may feel as though you're observing your own experiences from a distance. Such states of mind are typically fleeting, though certainly curious, and can lead you to ask some probing questions about who you might really be at some deeper level of existence.

Transcendental Tip—Sleep deprivation also may induce déjà vu experiences in which unfamiliar situations seem oddly familiar. If you *do* experience déjà vu during sleep deprivation, don't try to figure out why the experience seems familiar. Instead, imagine that you really have been "here" at another time. Indulge yourself in the fantasy and see what happens.

As you continue to experience sleep deprivation–induced states of consciousness, occasionally watch the clock and carry on with your quiet, but active, projects until sunrise. Then go out for a walk and observe the regular early-morning activities taking place around you. Finally, return for some breakfast. At this point you may either go to sleep or continue with the normal course of your day. Remember to be extra careful today if you have decided to go entirely without sleep.

DAY 12

A STAR
NAMED SUE

We've intentionally designed today's exercise for the evening so you can rest up after the sleep deprivation experience of Day 12. Tonight you'll take a more gentle approach to Higher Consciousness by focusing on the stars.

Begin this evening, after you've caught up on some sleep, by finding a quiet, dark, and secluded spot from which you can clearly observe the stars in the night sky. Stand with your head turned slightly upward, your legs slightly apart, and your hands at your sides. Take a deep breath and concentrate on a particular star.

Imagine that the star is a point of consciousness in space. Then envision that the center of your forehead and the star are connected by invisible lines of force. When you feel connected to the star, imagine that you are a constellation composed of individual stars located at different points all over your body. Then take another deep breath and, as you exhale, imagine that your body is dissolving. Only the stars marking your overall shape remain.

As you continue slowly inhaling and exhaling, imagine that the stars marking your shape mirror the positions of the stars overhead —as if the night sky is a reflection of yourself. Then imagine that *you* are a reflection of the stars. Alternately, imagine that you're in space looking back at Earth.

By imagining that you've let go of your physical form and can look back at your life on Earth, you may begin to see things with ever greater objectivity. As a result, you may reduce your level of stress, feel a deeper sense of connectedness to the cosmos, and gain insight into your true place in the universe.

DAY 13

QUIET
STORM

You will spend Day 13 in self-imposed silence. To succeed at this exercise, you must avoid talking to anyone at all. (Don't use a pen or word processor to write messages, either, since you would simply be substituting written words for verbal communication.) If you find it absolutely impossible to spend the entire day in silence, we suggest holding off on this exercise until you have time to do so.

You can practice this exercise at home, in a fancy midtown hotel, or in a remote rented cabin by a lake. Wherever you happen to be, however, *do not* watch television or listen to the radio. To avoid embarrassing situations, you may also find it helpful to explain your plans to a friend who can serve as your interpreter. If, for some reason, you are called upon to speak, your interpreter can simply answer for you.

If at all possible today, we suggest that you avoid people you know—with the exception of your interpreter. After all, those who don't know you will be less apt to find it strange that you aren't speaking and may just assume you can't talk. If you're feeling particularly adventurous, therefore, you may want to deliberately place yourself in completely unfamiliar surroundings for the duration of this experience.

Notice the way strangers act toward you when you first get to know one another without using words. Notice, also, how your perceptions of yourself and others may shift when freed of the pressures of verbal interaction.

> **Transcendental Tip**—An attorney friend of ours who practiced this exercise for an entire weekend was startled by the positive effect it had on his sense of reality and state of mind. He not only developed a number of new friendships without using words, but also became closer than ever to his confidante, who communicated with him on a deeply intuitive level for the first time.

> **Transcendental Tip**—As an even more intense variation on this exercise, you and your friend may decide to isolate yourselves from *all other people* and spend an entire weekend together in *mutual* silence. Instead of merely isolating yourselves indoors, moreover, you may find it worthwhile to visit some isolated outdoor location, such as a desert campsite or redwood forest.

DAY 14

THE WORLD
RUSHES IN

On Day 14 you will conclude the ''Broadcast News'' exercise you began on Day 8. By now you have probably been avoiding the news for almost a week. This afternoon, simply observe a variety of people in your neighborhood or office as they attend to the immediate concerns of their lives. As you observe the scene, ask yourself whether your perspective on humanity has at all changed during the past week. If it has, ask yourself how.

Late tonight, as on Day 8, turn off all the lights and turn on the 11:00 P.M. news. (Again, if you find it impossible to remain awake for the 11:00 news, you may substitute an earlier broadcast.) Once again, leave the sound turned off and sit at least several feet from the screen.

As you did before, watch the facial expressions of television news anchors introducing various stories and images. Notice the ways in which various stories lead into one another and into the commercials interspersed between them. Ask yourself whether the television reality you are observing bears any resemblance to the world you have been relating to all week.

Now gradually bring the television sound back up and listen to the news as it's being reported by the news anchors and commentators. As you listen, continue to experience a sense of distance from world events, much as you have done this past week. Notice how the words spoken by reporters may influence your feelings toward television images, and how your conscious interpretation of the images may seem to shift once you are distracted by the spoken words.

Congratulations! You've just completed Week Two of the Higher Consciousness Program.

WEEK TWO THE EVERYDAY MYSTIC

DAY 8 BROADCAST NEWS		**DAY 9** THE LIGHT FANTASTIC		
Turn off the lights and turn on the evening television news. Leave the sound turned off and focus on the facial expressions of the television news anchors. Pay close attention to the news and commercial images. Ask yourself how these images affect your view of yourself, human nature, and the world. After 30 minutes, go about your business as usual.	Before you fall asleep tonight, read ahead to the exercise for Day 10 so that you will be able to start as soon as you wake up in the morning. Spend the rest of this week deliberately avoiding contact with television news, weekly news magazines, or newspapers.	Begin the first thing in the morning, before you open your eyes. As you slowly come to consciousness, notice the way in which surrounding light filters through the surface of your eyelids. Slowly open your eyes and notice the layers of light and shadow in the room around you. Turn on the room light and notice how your perceptions and sense of reality shift the instant you throw the switch. Throughout the rest of your day, pay special attention to your ongoing interaction with light.	At sunset, stand outdoors or peer through your window and notice how your feelings shift as light gives way to darkness. After sunset, go for a walk and observe the way your sense of reality shifts with the darkness of night. Sit in an otherwise completely dark room with a burning candle a few feet away. Watch the flame and notice the moving patterns of light and shadow in the room around you. Blow out the candle and sit in the dark for at least 20 minutes.	

DAY 10 COLOR MY WORLD	**DAY 11** NIGHTHAWK

Notice the colors you choose to wear when you first get dressed in the morning and the colors you've used to decorate your home. As you leave home for the day, notice the color of the sky, the buildings, the sidewalks, and the vegetation. Notice the colors adorning animals, birds, and people you pass in the street. As much as possible, notice objects in terms of individual patches of color forming broader patterns of color in the world.	During the afternoon, choose a particular color and focus exclusively on its presence in your life. If you have time, you may then switch your focus to another color.	Practice this exercise only when sleeplessness won't interfere with your livelihood or safety or the safety of others. Conduct it at home or any-place else where you will be completely safe and undisturbed for the entire night. Vow to remain awake for at least 24 hours. To conserve energy, don't engage in strenuous physical activity. Use the time to pursue a quiet project that requires concentration.	As you feel the effects of sleep deprivation, find a comfortable place to sit and look directly at an illuminated watch or clock that has a second hand. Dim the lights and watch the clock. Relax and think of a significant upcoming event. Estimate the number of days before the event. Then estimate the number of hours, minutes, and seconds as well. Continue to watch the second hand sweeping around the clock.

	DAY 12 A STAR NAMED SUE		**DAY 13** QUIET STORM	
If you experience déjà vu, imagine that you really have been "here" at another time. Indulge yourself in the fantasy and see what happens. Occasionally watch the clock and carry on with your quiet, but active, projects until sunrise. After sunrise, go out for a walk and observe the early-morning activities taking place around you. Return home for some breakfast. Go to sleep or continue with the normal course of your day.	Rest up after the sleep deprivation experience of Day 11. This evening, find a quiet, dark, and secluded spot from which you can clearly observe the stars. Stand with your head turned slightly upward, your legs slightly apart, and your hands at your sides. Relax and concentrate on a particular star. Imagine that the star is a point of consciousness in space. Envision the center of your forehead and the star being connected by invisible lines of force.	Imagine that you are a constellation composed of stars located at different points all over your body. Then imagine that your body is dissolving and that only the stars marking your overall shape remain. Imagine that the stars marking your shape mirror the positions of the stars overhead. Then imagine that you are a reflection of the stars. Imagine that you're in space looking back at Earth. Then shift your focus back to your position on Earth, looking up at the stars.	Spend the day in self-imposed silence. To avoid embarrassing situations, explain your plans to a friend, who can serve as your interpreter. Notice the way strangers act toward you when you first get to know one another without using words. Notice how your perceptions of yourself and others shift when you are freed of verbal interaction.	

DAY 14
THE WORLD
RUSHES IN

This afternoon, observe a variety of people. Ask yourself whether your perspective toward humanity has changed during the past week.

Late tonight, turn off all the lights and turn on the evening television news. Once again, leave the sound turned off.

As you did before, watch the facial expressions of television news anchors. Notice the ways in which various stories lead into one another and into the commercials interspersed between them.

Ask yourself whether the television reality you are observing bears any resemblance to the world you have been relating to all week.

Gradually bring the television sound back up. Listen to the news being reported by news anchors and commentators. Continue to experience a sense of distance from world events, much as you have done throughout this past week.

Notice how the spoken words influence your feelings toward the television images.

WEEK THREE

INTERSECTING PLANES

WEEK THREE

•

I N T E R S E C T I N G
P L A N E S

*I*n Week Three of
the Higher Consciousness Program you should establish a sense of
mystical connection to other living things. Using a technique called
"transpersonal focusing," first of all, you will learn to psychologically merge with a range of animals from dogs and cats to elephants
and whales. You should also establish a mystical connection with
the insect world and even experience the feeling of "collective intelligence" as you envision yourself joining a colony of ants. After
you have "merged" with walking, breathing *creatures*, moreover,
you will work at establishing a sense of mystical communion with
plants.

Ultimately, Week Three exercises will teach you to "merge"
with a lover or friend. In one exercise you will mentally trade places
with your partner, envisioning your consciousness in his or her mind.
In another, you and your partner will make love while tapping the
heightened mystical sense that often accompanies sexual encounters.

Once you have mastered the transpersonal focusing techniques
presented in Week Three, a sense of higher connectedness should
carry you beyond your inner isolation toward a deeper sense of
compassion and appreciation for friends and strangers, insects and
animals, and the entire natural world.

Remember, there are those who might find the notion of merging
with trees and ants or "trading places" with friends unsettling. If
you count yourself among that small group, or begin to experience
even the slightest discomfort while practicing the exercises that fol-

low, proceed cautiously. Read through each exercise slowly and move forward only if you react to it with no fear or anxiety. Also proceed cautiously if you are using psychoactive drugs such as Thorazine or Stelazine, or if you have recently been subjected to electroconvulsive therapy or are otherwise under psychiatric or psychological care. In these instances, we urge you to continue with the Higher Consciousness Program only under the guidance of a licensed and qualified mental health professional.

Remember, transpersonal focusing is one of the most powerful —and gratifying—Higher Consciousness Program techniques. As you nurture your sense of connection to life, you should transcend the grind of everyday reality and come to see the world in a new, more brilliant, and infinitely more stimulating light.

DAY 15

TIGER'S EYE

How would your view of reality change if you could experience the world through the mind of a cat, dog, canary, or tiger? On Day 15, you will explore this question through a technique called "transpersonal focusing"—mentally trading places with a different form of life until you feel the distinctions between your individual identities blur.

You may practice this exercise with a wild animal, an animal in the zoo, or even the family pet. You might find it simplest to begin with a cat or dog and then move on to less domesticated animals as your experience mounts. Naturally, you'll want to be extremely careful if you apply the transpersonal focusing technique to a completely wild animal in its native surroundings. In that case, we recommend working with such relatively harmless creatures as penguins, rabbits, ducks, and frogs, rather than more dangerous species like panthers, rattlesnakes, and wolves. If you are an experienced scuba diver, this exercise is particularly effective when practiced underwater with some of the many friendly forms of life you're bound to encounter. But we wouldn't recommend ever trying this approach with a shark or any other dangerous form of sea life in the open water!

If you practice this technique at the zoo, be sure to keep your distance and be very discreet and sensitive to the needs of the animal you've chosen. We suggest selecting a time when the zoo is not crowded and the animals are therefore relatively calm.

> **Transcendental Tip**—We have had wonderful experiences in using this approach with both a black panther and a mountain gorilla on a rainy weekday afternoon at the San Francisco Zoo. The same approach tried on a busy Saturday in the Central Park Zoo, however, made a caged old lion extremely upset.

Begin by finding a domestic animal with which you feel at ease. Relax and sit in front of the animal so that you can easily look into each other's eyes. Do not, however, do anything that will make the animal feel nervous or tense. Take a deep breath. As you slowly exhale, look into the animal's eyes and imagine that a part of your awareness is being transmitted through your breath into the animal's mind. At the same time, watch the animal breathe and imagine that a part of its awareness is being transmitted into your mind.

Continue with this phase of the exercise for at least five minutes, until you feel the boundaries between your identity and that of the animal becoming less rigid. As time goes on, you may find the sense of connectedness becoming *so* intense that it feels powerfully real. You may also find yourself empathizing with the animal to such a large degree that it seems as if the two of you have mentally traded places. This is the height of transpersonal focusing, and can lead you to feel as though a part of you has stopped being human and become "something else." As a result, you may momentarily see your own identity—and the whole of reality—from a totally new point of view.

As you gradually let go of this experience and return to your more familiar self, you may find it worthwhile to consider how the forces of creation have coalesced to bring you and another species together to share this unique experience in this particular moment in space and time. You may even begin to recognize the parallels between the human and animal worlds.

Transcendental Tip—Once you have "merged" with a domestic animal, you'll be ready to explore the experience further with other
captive species and, finally, with animals in the wild. As you expand
your internal horizons, you may be startled to learn that "merging"
with different species may cause you to perceive reality in very different
ways.

DAY 16

EMPIRE OF
THE ANTS

On Day 16 you will carry the transpersonal focusing technique into the realm of the insect kingdom.

Transcendental Tip—A friend of ours recently practiced this exercise
late one evening in a phone booth at the end of a pier on the Outer
Banks of North Carolina. While he waited inside the well-lit booth for
a long-distance call to go through, a tiny winged insect of a kind he
had never seen came to rest at eye level on the outside of the glass.
The bug had black, bulging eyes and multicolored lines circling the
entire length of its body. It appeared to be looking him right in the
face.

As our friend watched the insect crawl along the outside of the
glass, he quickly found himself absorbed in its striking appearance
and fascinated by the fleeting interconnectedness of their mutual
realities. For a moment this focus became so intense that he almost
felt as though he had switched places with the creature and was
poised on the outside surface of the booth looking in at himself. The
experience provided him with a completely altered view of everyday
life.

To explore this type of experience yourself, choose a quiet location where you can sit and observe an individual insect. We suggest
that you practice this exercise at night, when you should find it fairly

easy to attract some sort of insect life to the outside surface of an illuminated window while you sit quietly inside.

Make yourself comfortable. Take a deep breath, slowly let it out, and allow yourself to relax. As you wait for a bug to land on the glass, imagine your awareness floating out through the window and into the surrounding darkness. How would you feel as a tiny speck of consciousness floating on transparent wings through space? How would the universe appear if you were so tiny that you could surround yourself in the petals of a single flower?

Continue focusing on these thoughts and images until you notice an insect landing on the outside of the glass. If the light has attracted more than a single insect to your window, focus on the one that is nearest to you. It is best if you can look the insect you select directly in the eyes. Since you and the bug both have faces, this initial level of contact should provide a sense of commonality with what may otherwise be experienced as a relatively unfamiliar form of life.

Continue to breathe slowly and deeply. As you exhale, imagine that a part of your awareness is flowing into the insect and observing your immediate surroundings from the other side of the glass. If you can maintain this perspective for about ten minutes, then the perceived distinction between you and the insect should become more fluid; it might even momentarily fade. As you inhale, focus once more on your human perspective. (If the insect you are observing happens to fly away from the window in the midst of the exercise, just imagine how it feels as it takes off, then allow your focus to return once again to your existence as a human being.)

Transcendental Tip—After you have practiced transpersonal focusing with an individual insect, you may wish to expand your focus to include several insects at once. You might, for instance, practice this exercise with the cockroaches crawling around your refrigerator late at night. You may even experiment by trying to merge your awareness with an entire *colony* of insects. An ideal subject for such an exercise would be a colony of ants. It is often said that insects reflect a unique dimension of collective intelligence. Imagine experiencing this type of intelligence—both as an individual ant and as an expression of the larger community within which each ant is a single unit or cell. As you complete this exercise, ask yourself whether any aspect of your be-

havior as a member of the broader human community resembles the
behavior of a single ant within an ant hill.

DAY 17

VEGETABLE
CONSCIOUSNESS

You have spent the past few days—not to men-
tion your entire life—exploring the byways of animal consciousness.
But on Day 17 you will mentally merge your consciousness with the
vegetable world as embodied by a tree.

For most of us, the idea of sharing a transpersonal experience
with a tree is hard to imagine. Trees, after all, do not appear to
reflect even the most rudimentary form of consciousness. Surely,
they seem far less conscious than the insects crawling around their
leaves. Trees are unquestionably alive, but their lives seem rooted
in consciousless cycles of growth and decay. Subjectively "merging" with a tree, therefore, may help you connect with a fundamental
level of the natural world.

We suggest that you begin by taking a walk through a forest,
park, or arboretum. Study the trees as you walk, choosing one that
appeals to you on both an aesthetic and emotional level. The tree
you choose should be close enough to other trees so that the branches
touch. It should not, however, be in a dangerous location (such as
the nether reaches of an inner-city park) or so close to other people
that you'll be distracted. Once you've chosen an appealing tree, sit
quietly on the ground next to it and relax.

As you sit beside your tree, take some time to appreciate its
singular existence. Notice the veins that thread across the leaves in
a delicate, life-sustaining design. Notice the way the leaves and
branches form intricate patterns across the background of the sky.
Even if there are millions of other trees of this same species in the
world, no other tree will ever form these identical patterns. Look
down at the ground around the base of the tree and notice how the

roots spread out below the surface. Notice, also, any decomposing leaves that may be completing their life cycles by returning to the soil.

Once you have achieved this initial focus, stand up, press your body against the tree, and embrace the trunk with your arms. Take a deep breath. As you exhale, imagine your body merging with the body of the tree. See your legs becoming part of the root system, your torso becoming part of the trunk, and your head and fingers becoming one with the branches and leaves.

Now feel water flowing up from the ground into the tree and your body at once. Envision the water flowing through your arms, legs, fingers, and toes; envision it flowing through the tree's trunk, branches, and leaves.

Now press one ear against your tree and imagine the sound of water flowing up through the trunk to the leaves. At the same time, imagine vibrations moving through your entire body. Let yourself vibrate in rhythm with your tree and all the trees until you feel a sense of connectedness to the natural world.

To enhance this sense of integration, envision the roots, leaves, and branches of your tree spreading out and connecting with other trees around you. Imagine that these are your own roots, leaves, and branches, and that *you* are also spreading out below the soil and across the air. Feel yourself intermingling so closely with the trees around you that you no longer feel like a single tree within a larger landscape, but rather like a *colony* of trees with many individual trunks and centers. Your envisioned individual participation in this arboreal tapestry should help you feel a connection to all living things.

To complete this exercise, continue breathing in and out. As you inhale, imagine the whole of nature entering your being on a deep, inner level. As you exhale, imagine yourself contributing a part of your innermost self to the larger universe around you. Gradually let go of the tree and, as you move away from it, feel your consciousness once more centered within yourself. Before you continue with your day, spend one last minute appreciating the unique and changing patterns of the trees.

Transcendental Tip—When practicing "Vegetable Consciousness," do not imagine yourself in the form of a half-human, half-plant crea-ture resembling the apple trees in *The Wizard of Oz*. Instead, just imagine what it might be like to live with no conscious thought patterns as you know them. Allow yourself to feel this experience as deeply as possible.

DAY 18

THE FAR SIDE

What would your life be like if you were a character in a comic strip? Suppose your life were really a collection of scenes from the Sunday funnies, or something out of a Saturday morning cartoon? Would you approach your experience of everyday reality any differently if you knew that whatever was happening to you was intended purely for the entertainment of people in another reality, whom you've never even met? On Day 18, you will explore this question in the hope of gaining a greater perspective toward the people and events in your life.

Begin by spending an hour or two enjoying a collection of cartoons by your favorite artist. (There are many published collections of such cartoons available at your local bookstore.) Our own particular favorite for this exercise is Gary Larson's wonderful series, "The Far Side," although we also highly recommend "Bloom County," "Herman," "B.C.," "Blondie," "Ernie," "Outland," and anything by Charles Addams, Gahan Wilson, Edward Gorey, or George Booth. To enhance the atmosphere for this particular exercise, we also recommend playing a videotape or actual broadcast of any humorous collection of Saturday morning cartoons in the background. Such cartoon shows as "The Jetsons," "The Flintstones," "The Bugs Bunny Show," and "The Road Runner" would be ideal. For the purpose of this exercise, however, please avoid such militaristic cartoon show selections as "G.I. Joe," "Thundercats," and "Teenage Mutant Ninja Turtles."

As you leaf through the collection of printed cartoons you've selected, allow your imagination to become fully immersed in the warped or surrealistic reality inhabited by the cartoon characters. Are there elements of this cartoon reality that resonate with more familiar experiences that have happened in your own life? Can you empathize with the characters, or identify with the feelings and ideas of the artist who created them?

Every so often, take a break and shift your focus of attention to the cartoon show playing in the background. Imagine that you are one of the characters on the screen. How do you feel about yourself in the role of the character you've selected?

After you've immersed yourself in the world of your chosen comic strip, focus on the character with whom you most deeply identify and imagine you have taken over his or her role. Close your eyes and "feel" your three-dimensional form flatten out to the two-dimensional reality of the page. Imagine your facial features taking on the surrealistic tones of comic strip life, and see yourself coping with the character's traumas, foibles, and outrageous good or bad luck. After 10 to 20 minutes, envision yourself returning to your customary 3-D form.

> **Transcendental Tip**—In the future, as you go through the inevitable stresses of life, ask yourself whether somebody or something, some-where in the universe, might be busting a gut with laughter over your most private predicaments in the same way that you sometimes laugh at the two-dimensional characters in cartoons. Posing this question will help you step back and view yourself more objectively. Once you come to appreciate the somewhat surrealistic quality of everyday existence, you may develop a lighter, more existential attitude toward life.

DAY 19

BODY
SWAPPING

On Days 19 through 21, you will practice trans-personal focusing with another person. We suggest that you share the exercises with a very close and trusted friend or, preferably, with your lover. It would be ideal if the person you choose is also participating in the Higher Consciousness Program.

Begin by sitting with your partner in a private and quiet indoor place where you won't be disturbed for at least an hour. Take some time to relax and get comfortable together. Play some calming or romantic music in the background and share a light meal of some sliced fruit and a small glass of juice or wine. Sharing food is a traditional way of establishing a bond with one another, though you shouldn't eat so much on this particular occasion that you'll become full or distracted from the transpersonal focusing exercise itself.

Once you have completed your light repast, sit on the floor facing your companion; ideally, the two of you should be a few feet apart. From this point until the end of the exercise, you and your partner may not talk. The room should be moderately lit—not too bright or dark—and you should continue playing quiet music in the background. Begin by simply noticing your own and your partner's breathing for three or four minutes.

You and your partner should now synchronize the rhythm of your breathing, inhaling and exhaling together. As you breathe, look deeply into your partner's eyes and remember the feelings you had when you looked into your own eyes during the mirror exercise ("Fantastic Voyage") of Week One. Imagine that your partner's eyes are really your own, and that you are sitting across from your present position, looking back at yourself. Maintain this focus and synchronize your breathing until you momentarily feel the psychological separation between you and your partner dissolve. Now imagine that your partner no longer exists as a distinct and separate individual, but rather is merely another aspect of your own existence.

Then, imagine that you have just come into existence in this moment and that everything outside this room is an illusion. Imagine, also, that everything about your partner's outside life is similarly an illusion. Mentally reject any perception of your partner's life experience as separate from your own.

Finally, look deeply into your partner's eyes and say to yourself, "This is another aspect of myself." Repeat these words several times in your thoughts, until you feel their deeper meaning sink in. You and your partner may communicate the fact that you have completed this portion of the exercise by closing your eyes and lowering your heads.

When you've both finished, sit with your eyes closed and allow your breathing to return to normal. Slowly reassimilate your sense of self as a separate individual. Also allow yourself to accept the apparent reality of your memories and your everyday life. When you feel that you have regained a sense of equilibrium, open your eyes and look at your partner. When your partner is ready and also looks up, you may both feel free to discuss the experiences you have just had.

> **Transcendental Tip**—Do not, under any circumstances, carry out this exercise while drunk or under the influence of psychoactive or so-called recreational drugs.

DAY 20

ECSTASY

The "Ecstasy" exercise is purely sexual. If carried out thoroughly, it should help you expand your sense of connection to your partner. It will also add a more intimate dimension to your higher consciousness explorations.

> **Transcendental Tip**—Today's exercise requires that you feel completely comfortable and open with your partner on a sexual level. If you are not, for any reason, able to comfortably carry out the sexual activities we will be discussing at this point in the Higher Consciousness Program, you may substitute any of the other exercises you have already practiced. However, we do suggest that, if possible, you share any substitute exercise with a friend.

If you have elected to carry out the sexual aspects of this program, please begin by finding a cozy and private place where you can be alone with your lover for at least several hours. We suggest that the place you choose be equipped with a comfortable bed—unless you personally prefer to make love on the living room floor or the kitchen table. It would be especially enjoyable to carry out today's exercise in the course of a romantic weekend at some out-of-the-way retreat.

Once you have chosen a special environment, retire there and share a light meal of some sliced fruit and a small glass of juice or wine. Play some romantic music quietly in the background and lower the lights to a soothing level. When you and your lover have completed the meal, light a few candles and switch off any electrical lights. Then stand up and slowly undress each other by candlelight, taking care to touch only one another's clothing but *not* any part of your bare bodies.

When you are both completely naked, stand face-to-face, as close to one another as possible without touching. Feel the warmth emanating from your lover's body and notice the shadows playing across his or her skin in the flickering light. Notice any feelings of sexual arousal that you may be experiencing. Tell your lover, in specific detail, why you find him or her physically attractive. You might say, for example, ''Your prominent nose makes a powerful, erotic statement,'' or ''I love the way your shoulders slope down into those slim, graceful arms.''

Sit down and face one another on the bed or floor. Move your hands slowly above the surface of your lover's body, still without actually making physical contact. Then allow your lover to do the same to you. As your lover's hands move around you, imagine that you can feel his or her hands stimulating a deepening sense of sexual excitement throughout your entire body.

Now, much like yesterday, cease all talk and look into your lover's eyes. Notice the rhythm of his or her breath and your own for three or four minutes. As you did yesterday, synchronize the rhythm of your breathing, inhaling and exhaling together. As you breathe, look deeply into your partner's eyes and remember the feelings you had when you looked into your own eyes during Week One of the program. Imagine that your partner's eyes are really your own and that you are sitting across from your present position, looking back at yourself. Maintain this focus and synchronize your breathing until you momentarily feel the psychological separation between you and your partner dissolve. Now imagine that your partner no longer exists as a distinct and separate individual, but rather is merely another aspect of you.

Now, with your eyes still open, gently touch your lover's face and imagine that you are physically exploring another aspect of your own existence. Allow your lover to touch you in the same fashion. Gradually allow your caresses to roam more freely and sexually around your lover's body. As you do so, continue focusing on the idea of your lover as another aspect of yourself, and touch him or her in special ways that you sense—on an intuitive level—would be especially pleasurable. At the same time, intuitively respond to your lover's touch until your mutual sexual arousal increases and you spontaneously find yourselves making love.

> **Transcendental Tip**—To heighten your sexual sensitivity, we suggest that you abstain from sexual intercourse for a day or two before you carry out today's session.

DAY 21

THE CENTERED SELF

Today's exercise will help you resume a centered sense of self following the emotional and physical intensity of the past two days. Spend two or three hours entirely alone today, in some natural or beautiful setting that makes you feel calm within yourself. You may, for example, choose to walk on a deserted beach, wander through a botanical garden, row a boat across a lake, or go for a walk in the woods or along the edge of a river. You may also walk through an art museum or a large cathedral or synagogue in the city where you live.

Use this time to reflect upon how your sense of yourself, the world, and reality itself has been influenced by your connection to your lover, with whom you have shared the transpersonal focusing exercises of the past two days.

After you have spent sufficient time alone, have your special friend or lover meet you at this quiet locale. Then set out to explore this place together. As you do so, share with your partner the special thoughts you have about him or her. Notice how your experience of the previous days—and even hours—seem so much a part of the past, even though relatively little time has gone by. Consider how, in the future that will begin the moment you leave this place, the memory of having been here with your friend or lover may be something you each look back on for the rest of your lives.

Following your walk, take a short break with your partner and enjoy a pleasant snack or meal. Use this time to catch up on how you both feel about the way things are going in your individual lives. If the timing is right, and if this seems appropriate to your relationship, make passionate love at some point before the day is up. Reaffirm your mutual appreciation for one another's unique existence on this planet and in each other's lives.

Remember, it's time to celebrate! You've just completed Week Three of the Higher Consciousness Program.

WEEK THREE INTERSECTING PLANES

DAY 15 TIGER'S EYE		**DAY 16** EMPIRE OF THE ANTS	
Find a domestic animal with which you feel at ease. Relax and sit in front of the animal so that you can easily look into each other's eyes. Do not do anything that will make the animal feel uncomfortable, tense, or nervous. Take a deep breath. As you exhale, look into the animal's eyes and imagine that part of your awareness is being transmitted through your breath into the animal's mind. Watch the animal breathe and imagine part of its awareness is also being transmitted into your mind.	Continue with this phase of the exercise for five minutes, until you feel the boundaries between your identity and that of the animal becoming less rigid. Gradually return to your more familiar sense of self. Consider how the forces of creation have coalesced to bring you and another species together to share this unique experience in this particular moment in space and time.	Choose a quiet location next to a lighted window at night and wait for an individual insect to land on the glass. Imagine your awareness floating out through the window and into the surrounding darkness. Continue focusing on these thoughts and images until an insect lands on the outside of the glass. Focus on the insect, looking it directly in the eyes.	Imagine that part of your awareness is flowing into the insect and observing your surroundings from the other side of the glass. Maintain this perspective for about ten minutes. If the insect you are observing flies away from the window in the midst of the exercise, imagine how it feels as it takes off. Focus once again on your human perspective.

DAY 17
VEGETABLE CONSCIOUSNESS

Take a walk through a forest, park, or arboretum. Study the trees, choosing one that appeals to you. Sit quietly on the ground next to it and relax.

Sit beside your tree and take time to appreciate its singular existence. Notice the veins that thread across the leaves, and the intricate patterns formed by the leaves and branches against the background of the sky.

Look at the ground around the base of the tree. Notice any decomposing leaves. Notice how the roots spread out below the surface.

Stand up and press your body against the tree. Embrace the trunk with your arms. Take a deep breath.

As you exhale, imagine your body merging with the body of the tree. Press one ear against the tree and imagine the sound of water flowing up through the trunk to the leaves. Imagine similar vibrations moving through your entire body.

Allow yourself to feel a sense of connectedness to the natural world.

Gradually let go of the tree and, as you move away from it, feel your consciousness once more becoming centered within yourself.

Spend one last minute appreciating the unique and changing patterns of the trees around you.

DAY 18
THE FAR SIDE

Spend an hour or two enjoying a collection of print cartoons. Play animated cartoons in the background. Allow your imagination to become fully immersed in the reality inhabited by the cartoon characters.

Focus on a cartoon character with whom you personally identify and imagine you have taken over his or her role. Close your eyes and "feel" your three-dimensional form flatten out to the two-dimensional reality of the cartoon.

DAY 19
BODY
SWAPPING

Imagine yourself coping with the character's traumas, foibles, and outrageous good or bad luck. After 10 to 20 minutes, envision yourself returning to your customary 3-D form.

Ask yourself whether somebody or something, somewhere in the universe, might be laughing over your private predicaments in the same way that you sometimes laugh at the two-dimensional characters in cartoons.

Sit with a close friend or lover in a private and quiet indoor place where you won't be disturbed for at least an hour.

Relax and get comfortable together. Play calming or romantic music in the background and share a light meal. Dim the lights.

Sit on the floor facing your companion. From this point until the end of the exercise, you and your partner may not talk.

Synchronize the rhythm of your breathing.

Look deeply into your partner's eyes. Imagine that your partner's eyes are really your own, and that you are sitting across from your present position, looking back at yourself.

Maintain this focus and synchronize your breathing until you momentarily feel as though you and your partner no longer exist as distinct and separate individuals.

Imagine that you have just come into existence and that everything outside this room is an illusion. Imagine that everything you remember about your partner's outside life is also an illusion.

Mentally reject any perception of your partner's life experience as separate from your own.

Slowly reassimilate your sense of self as a separate individual. Also acknowledge the apparent reality of your memories and everyday life.

DAY 20
ECSTASY

If you have elected to carry out the sexual aspects of this program, find a private place where you can be alone with your lover for at least several hours.

Share a light meal, play some romantic music, and lower the lights to a soothing level. Then light a few candles and switch off any electrical lights.

Stand up and slowly undress each other by candlelight, taking care to touch only one another's clothing but not any part of your bare bodies.

Stand face-to-face as close to one another as possible without touching. Notice any feelings of sexual arousal.

Tell your lover, in specific detail, why you find him or her physically attractive.

Sit down and face one another on the bed or floor. Move your hands slowly above the surface of your lover's body, without making physical contact. Allow your lover to do the same to you. Imagine that you can feel your lover's hands stimulating a deepening sense of sexual excitement throughout your body.

Repeat the transpersonal focusing exercise of Day 19. Then gently touch your lover's face and imagine that you are physically exploring another aspect of your own existence. Allow your lover to touch you in the same fashion.

Gradually allow your caresses to roam more freely and sexually around your lover's body. Continue focusing on the idea of your lover as another aspect of yourself, and touch him or her in special, sexual ways.

Respond to your lover's touch until your mutual sexual arousal increases and you spontaneously find yourselves making love.

DAY 21
THE CENTERED
SELF

Spend two or three hours entirely alone in a natural or beautiful setting that makes you feel calm within yourself.

Reflect upon how your sense of yourself, the world, and reality has been influenced by your connection to your lover, or the friend with whom you have shared the transpersonal focusing exercises of the past two days.

Have your special friend or lover meet you at this quiet locale. Then explore this place together, sharing with your partner the special thoughts you have about him or her.

Notice how your experiences of the previous hours and days are now a part of the past. Consider how the memory of having been here with your friend or lover may be something you both look back on for the rest of your lives.

Following your walk, take a short break with your partner and enjoy a pleasant snack or meal. Use this time to catch up on how you both feel about the way things are going in your individual lives.

If the timing is right, and if this seems appropriate, make passionate love with your partner at some point before the day is up. Reaffirm your mutual appreciation for one another's unique existence on this planet and in each other's lives.

WEEK FOUR

TRAVELS THROUGH SPACE AND TIME ●

WEEK FOUR

•

You visit a new friend in a strange city for the first time. As you talk over coffee, a mystical sensation creeps over you. You have, you feel certain, been here before.

This compelling feeling, known as déjà vu, has fascinated human beings for thousands of years. Many contemporary scientists attribute the sensation to exhaustion and stress or to nerve cells misfiring in the brain. New Age theorists contend that déjà vu is spurred by past life memories, or the suddenly triggered recollection of a precognitive dream.

We make no effort to explain the phenomenon here, but there's one thing of which we feel certain: With the proper training, most people can learn to experience the mystical sense of déjà vu at will. All that's needed is a series of powerful techniques known as "spatial and temporal shifting," in which you may consciously alter your psychological perspective toward the past, present, and future, and consciously manipulate your internal perception of space and time.

As you learn to perfect these focusing techniques, you will render your perception of space and time far more fluid, and conventional boundaries dividing past and future, near and far, will appear to fade. As a result, you will be able to mentally traverse the globe, commune with your future self, and evoke the emotional presence of the inner child you thought you'd left behind. As you experience the altered states induced by temporal and spatial shifting, moreover, you should at once enhance your sense of wonder and your sense of objectivity toward space and time. By viewing these essential elements of reality from a more transcendent perspective, you should gain a greater sense of clarity and appreciation toward both the transitory and eternal elements of your life.

We hope you're enjoying yourself and getting something meaningful and positive from the Higher Consciousness Program. As you complete Week Four—and the rest of your life—remember that Higher Consciousness may best be experienced not as a bolt from the heavens, but rather as a subtly heightened awareness of your own existence and your place in the world and the universe beyond.

DAY 22

DÉJÀ VU

Today you will attempt to transcend your linear experience of time by connecting with your future self. Begin the exercise early in the day, just as you are leaving the inside of your home to run some errands, pulling out of the driveway to go to work, or taking the bus or subway to your office. Choose a particular spot on this outbound phase of your journey and imagine yourself passing this same location, moving in the opposite direction, on the way home. As you drive down the freeway, for example, envision your future self driving down the opposite side of the freeway in the return direction. Or, as you begin pulling out of the driveway in the morning, imagine that you can actually see your future self pulling back into the driveway in the early evening.

As you conjure this image, imagine communicating directly with your future self. Does your future self know something that the present-day you has not yet discovered? If you are on your way to an important meeting, for example, imagine yourself returning long after the meeting is over. Can you "see" the expression you'll have on your face as you're returning home? Can you sense any of the feelings you'll be having about how the meeting went? Ask your future self, in your thoughts, if there is anything it would be helpful for you to know in order to mentally prepare yourself for the meeting to follow.

Complete this exercise during your return trip. As you pass the same spot where you first began the exercise earlier in the day, compare your actual feelings with your earlier impressions. Imagine that you are passing your earlier self traveling in the opposite direction, and communicating with your past self about your knowledge of the future.

> ***Transcendental Tip***—This exercise can be practiced on an ongoing basis. You may find it particularly useful as an aid in dealing with anticipated stress.

DAY 23

YESTERDAY'S CHILD

Today you will communicate on a deep, internal level with remembered impressions of yourself in the distant past. By communicating directly with the child still within, you can rediscover dreams and goals that have long seemed lost. You can also learn to share with your childhood self the greater wisdom of the adult you have become.

To begin today's exercise, choose a spot that was especially significant to you as a child and, if possible, go there. If the spot is too far away to visit conveniently, choose a substitute site that reminds you of the original. Or, simply sit alone in a quiet and dimly lit environment and visit the place in your imagination. The place you select does not need to be one you visited on a daily basis. A church, an attic room, or possibly the home of a favorite relative would be suitable locations, as would a playground, museum, doughnut shop, pizzeria, or bowling alley.

If the location you select is a large building, choose a more or less secluded place within where you can sit quietly without being interrupted. Be certain, however, that the exact spot you select is someplace where you spent at least one particularly thoughtful occasion alone as a child.

Take a deep breath, relax, and recall how you felt when you first visited this place as a child. Instead of merely analyzing your childhood feelings from the viewpoint of an adult, however, try to relive your childhood experience. Try, as best you can, to focus on whatever questions were most important to you then.

Now, imagine that time as we normally think of it does not exist, and that you can communicate directly with your childhood self. Exchange viewpoints with each other: As the child, tell the adult things that may have been forgotten, revealing your deepest desires and goals. As the adult, share with the child what you now know about life. Ask the child you once were to recall some worthwhile aspects of your personality or inner experience with which you have lost touch.

As you practice this exercise, you may experience a sense of timelessness. You may, for instance, feel the apparent separation between past and present fade—as though the child and the adult were alive inside you at once. The child's insights may help soften the hardened or jaded parts of your adult personality. The adult point of view may help resolve conflicted childhood feelings.

Complete this exercise by giving a gift to the childhood part of yourself. Was there some toy you wanted as a child but couldn't have? Do you recall a treasured childhood possession you long ago lost? Was there some special place you were never able to go? A snack or dessert you longed for? Whatever that ancient longing, indulge yourself now.

Transcendental Tip—You may enhance your experience of this exercise by playing music that you originally heard as a child. Allow the music to remind you of your childhood and use it to emotionally connect you with your own remembered past.

DAY 24

BACK TO
THE FUTURE

On Day 24 of the Higher Consciousness Program, visit a spot that is especially significant to you now. Then vow to return to this place at some distant point in your future. The exact date may be left open, or you may want to specify a particular time, say New Year's Eve in five years. You may also decide to return to the same location at planned or irregular intervals throughout your life, establishing a kind of psychological sacred ground from which to gain insights into your worldly existence.

Take some time to relax in the place you have chosen, and quietly reflect on those matters that are of deepest personal concern to you in your present life. Are you dissatisfied with your job? Unhappy in a relationship? Afraid to try something new? Dealing with some overwhelming burden?

Now imagine yourself at this same spot in the distant future. Review your present concerns with the insights you believe you may gain in future years. If you feel frustrated about your present situation, the insights from your future self may help alleviate some of your tension or unhappiness. As you envision an older and wiser self, you will be less likely to feel stuck. You may also experience sensations of timelessness, not unlike those you experienced on Days 22 and 23.

Transcendental Tip—As you become more experienced at Week Four techniques, you may eventually want to bring your past, present, and future selves together in your mind's eye. To do so, visit your special childhood spot and simultaneously invoke your childhood self and the self you expect to become in the future.

DAY 25

THE ROAD
NOT TAKEN

Among the most significant places in your life are those that symbolize a turning point—when you rejected one major choice or direction in favor of another. This symbolic location can be one in which you once escaped death, experienced personal tragedy or triumph, or made a dramatic, life-changing decision.

On Day 25 you will focus on such a place, achieving a greater sense of your personal destiny in the process. Begin by returning to some psychologically significant site, representing a point at which your existence came to a symbolic fork in the road and you took one life path rather than another. (If you cannot physically return to such a site, substitute a similar spot to which you have easy access.)

Once you arrive at your chosen spot, find a comfortable place to sit, relax, and focus on the surroundings. Allow your impressions to carry you back to an earlier time, during a major life event at this same locale. Recall, in vivid detail, what these surroundings looked like during that earlier period. Tapping into your innermost feelings, recall the events and people crucial to your life at that time. Don't just analyze your feelings or review them from a detached distance. Instead, allow yourself to reexperience the past on as deep an emotional level as is comfortable and possible.

After you reexperience your past emotions, reflect on how events in your life have since evolved. As you have done in past exercises, imagine communicating with your past self and sharing the knowledge and wisdom of your accumulated life experience.

Finally, try to achieve some sense of emotional detachment from the turning point upon which you are focusing. Then focus on the sequence of events that have unfolded from the time of the turning point to the present. How did the decisions you made back then lead to your current situation? What aspects of your life—and the lives of others—might be different now had you taken an alternate path?

Conclude this exercise by conjuring the images of your past, future, and present selves all at once. Then allow these images to dissolve in a mental mist. As they fade from your conscious awareness, walk away from the symbolic spot you have chosen and psychologically leave it behind. Focus on your present self and on turning points yet to come.

> **Transcendental Tip**—You may also practice this exercise with a partner, especially if the two of you have shared a turning point in your life. One couple we know, for example, practiced this exercise together following the San Francisco earthquake of October 1989. Shortly before the earthquake occurred they had seriously considered moving to a spacious apartment in the Marina District with a beautiful view of the Golden Gate Bridge. One of them concluded, however, that the building would not withstand a major earthquake, and therefore convinced the other to take a more expensive apartment built on bedrock a short distance away.
>
> When the earthquake hit a month later, the first building collapsed and burned in a deadly inferno that made headlines in newspapers all over the country. The couple later stood at the edge of the smoldering ashes, feeling deeply grateful for having narrowly escaped this tragedy. They experienced a deepened sense of appreciation for one another and for the extra time they felt they had been given to make positive contributions in their lives.
>
> **Transcendental Tip**—If you have any doubts about your psychological ability to handle this experience, we urge you to check with your doctor or therapist and consider carrying out this exercise only under clinical supervision.

DAY 26

THE FORGOTTEN
CITY

During the past four days, you've connected with your past and future selves, transcending the linear experience of time. On Days 26 and 27, you will expand this perspective to include other people in the distant past and future.

On Day 26, you will focus on the site of a condemned building. Your goal: to experience the relationship between your contemporary existence and the lives of other people in the distant past.

To start, locate a building currently undergoing demolition. (If you cannot find such a building locally, you may substitute one that is seriously deteriorating because of natural decay and neglect.)

Position yourself at a safe distance from the demolition site and observe the building as it is slowly torn down. Imagine how permanent the building must have seemed to the people who once lived or worked there. Pay attention to the relationship between the different floors and rooms. Don't they seem close to one another once the outer walls are gone? Think about all the people who have lived or worked in the building throughout its existence. Imagine their worldviews, their occupations, and even the activities and conversations they conducted in the building when it was new.

> **Transcendental Tip**—Even the most seemingly constant aspects of your environment are only temporary, part of the continuum that constitutes history itself. As you accept the ultimate impermanence of even large-scale everyday objects, such as buildings, you may gain greater awareness of the impermanent nature of your own everyday existence. You therefore may be more willing to take intelligent risks and make positive changes in your life.

> **Transcendental Tip**—In a variation on the exercise above, you may decide to focus on some historically significant place, such as the ruins of ancient Rome or Philadelphia's Independence Hall.

DAY 27

URBAN
RENEWAL

On Day 27, you will focus on a new building under construction. The goal: to explore your relationship with future generations.

As you observe the construction process, consider that the workers are not merely raising another structure but are creating a reality for those who will live or work in the new building. Who will live here? What will they say to one another? How might their personal views of the world differ from yours?

Make an agreement with yourself to explore the interior of the new building once it is completed. When you visit the finished building, imagine that you are leaving a mental trace of your own life experience for future generations to explore in later years.

Complete this exercise by imagining this building as it will look in the far future, when in the process of being torn down, perhaps to make way for yet another development project. What will the environment surrounding this site be like at that time? What will future generations think of this now-brand-new building when it too becomes an antique relic of the past?

DAY 28

STARRY, STARRY NIGHT

The final exercise of Week Four will help you transcend your earthbound concept of space and time. Before you begin, familiarize yourself with the constellations in the night sky. To do so, simply visit your local planetarium or study an appropriate chart or book. It would also be particularly helpful to learn to identify a single constellation, perhaps one with which you feel a special affinity.

After you have done your homework, find a comfortable spot in an open clearing away from city lights: the roof of a house or building, a deck cantilevered over the Pacific, or a grassy meadow would work well. Now relax and look up at the constellations. First, imagine yourself at this same spot on prehistoric Earth. As you envision a nearby community of hunter-gatherers or long-lost species of animals, look up at the sky. After a minute or two, imagine yourself viewing the same configuration of stars from this same spot, but thousands of years in the future. As you look up at your constellation, conjure a detailed vision of the future Earth. Remember, it doesn't matter whether you picture a burnt-out shell of a planet or a utopia of gardens, towers, and jet packs, so long as you have traveled—in your mind's eye—fast forward through the years.

> *Transcendental Tip*—Keep in mind that people have viewed these same constellations for millions of years. These constellations will also be visible long after you have left the spot you occupy now. In fact, they will be visible long after your life has come to an end. Consider, also, that the starlight you are seeing really took thousands of years to reach you. You are therefore seeing the stars as they appeared in a distant place thousands of years ago. What's more, it will be thousands of years before anyone on Earth can look up at the night sky and see the stars as they really exist today.

Finally, as you watch the constellations, think about some distant place you would like to visit. Ask yourself how these same constellations would look above that far-off locale right now. Then imagine yourself at that far away spot *and* your present location simultaneously. See your consciousness drifting up from both places and connecting with your favorite constellation above. Finally, sense your consciousness moving back and forth, again and again, from the constellation to either locale.

Continue practicing this exercise until the sensation that you exist in a single place or time starts to fade.

> *Transcendental Tip*—The grandeur and immensity of the night sky should induce a sense of wonder at the world and a serene acceptance of your place within it. As you mentally traverse the universe, the apparent limitations of space and time may seem less confining than before.

> *Transcendental Tip*—You may also use the "Starry, Starry Night" technique to form a long-distance connection with a partner. You and your partner must simply agree to gaze at the same star patterns at the same time from your mutual locations. As you both focus on the chosen stars, imagine that you are actually side by side. Then consider this: Since you are both viewing the same star patterns from the surface of the same tiny dot in space, you are, in a sense,

together—regardless of the relatively small distance between you in this remote corner of the universe.

Transcendental Tip—The "Starry, Starry Night" technique can provide a particularly effective focus on an annual holiday, such as your birthday or New Year's Eve. For instance, on the stroke of midnight on New Year's Eve, simply gaze up at the constellations. As you do so, recall the past year. Then see yourself looking up at these same constellations a year, and then a decade or more, from now. Feel the relationship between the changing patterns of your life and the constant design of the night sky.

It's time to congratulate yourself. You have just completed Week Four of the Higher Consciousness Program.

WEEK FOUR TRAVELS THROUGH SPACE AND TIME

DAY 22 DÉJÀ VU	DAY 23 YESTERDAY'S CHILD		DAY 24 BACK TO THE FUTURE
Choose a spot and imagine yourself passing this same location, moving in the opposite direction, later today.

Imagine communicating with your future self.

During your return trip, as you pass the spot where you first began the exercise earlier in the day, imagine that you are passing your earlier self traveling in the opposite direction.

Imagine communicating with your past self about your knowledge of the future. | Choose a spot that was significant to you as a child and, if possible, go there. If the spot is too far away to visit conveniently, choose a substitute site that reminds you of the original or visit the place in your imagination.

Relax and recall how you felt when you first visited this place as a child. Mentally relive your childhood experience.

Imagine that time as we normally think of it does not exist, and that you can communicate directly with your childhood self. | Give a gift to the childhood part of yourself. | Visit a spot that is significant to you now. Vow to return to this place at some distant point in the future.

Relax in the place you have chosen. Quietly reflect on those matters that are of deepest personal concern to you in your present life.

Imagine yourself at this same spot in the distant future. Imagine communicating with your future self and reviewing your present concerns with the insights you believe you may gain in future years. |

DAY 25 THE ROAD NOT TAKEN		*DAY 26* THE FORGOTTEN CITY
Return to a psychologically significant site, one that represents a turning point in your life. If you cannot physically return to such a site, substitute a similar spot to which you have easy access. Find a comfortable place to sit, relax, and focus on your surroundings. Allow your impressions to carry you back to an earlier time, during a major life event at this (or a similar) locale.	Reexperience your past emotions. Reflect on how events in your life have since evolved. Imagine communicating with your past self and sharing the knowledge and wisdom of your accumulated life experience. Allow yourself to achieve some sense of emotional detachment from the turning point upon which you are focusing. Focus on the sequence of events that have unfolded from the time of the turning point to the present.	Conjure images of your past, future, and present selves all at once. Allow these images to dissolve in a mental mist. As they fade from your awareness, walk away from the symbolic spot you have chosen and psychologically leave it behind. Focus on your present self and on turning points yet to come.	Locate a building that is currently undergoing demolition. Position yourself at a safe distance from the demolition site and observe the building as it is torn down. Imagine how permanent the building must have seemed to the people who once lived or worked there. Consider their view of reality and the nature of their everyday lives.

DAY 27
URBAN RENEWAL

DAY 28
STARRY,
STARRY NIGHT

Locate a building that is under construction.

Position yourself at a safe distance and observe the construction process. Consider what everyday reality will be like inside the building for the people who will live or work there.

Vow to explore the interior of the building once it is completed.

Eventually visit the finished building. Imagine that you are leaving a mental trace of your own life experience behind for future generations.

Imagine this building as it will look in the far future, when in the process of being torn down. What will the environment surrounding this site be like at that time? What will everyday reality be like for future generations when this now-brand-new building is an antique relic of the distant past?

Familiarize yourself with the constellations in the night sky. Learn to identify a single constellation with which you feel a special affinity.

After you have done your homework, find a comfortable spot in an open clearing away from city lights. Relax and look up at the constellations.

Imagine yourself at this same spot on prehistoric Earth. After a minute or two, imagine yourself viewing the same configuration of stars from this same spot thousands of years in the future.

Consider that the starlight you are seeing really took thousands of years to reach you.

Think about a distant place that you would like to visit. Ask yourself how these same constellations would look above that far-off locale. Imagine yourself at that distant spot and your present location simultaneously.

See your con-
sciousness
drifting up
from both
places and
connecting
with your fa-
vorite constel-
lation above.
Sense your
consciousness
moving back
and forth,
again and
again, from the
constellation to
either locale.

Continue prac-
ticing this ex-
ercise until the
sensation that
you exist in a
single place or
time starts to
fade.

Assume your
familiar per-
spective to-
ward mundane
reality.

DAYS
29 AND 30

THE OTHER SIDE •

DAYS
29 AND 30

•

T H E   O T H E R   S I D E

DAY 29

THE GRATEFUL DEAD

On Day 29 we would like you to visit a cemetery, ideally one that includes gravesites from many different historical eras.

Transcendental Tip—We recently carried out this exercise in a town graveyard associated with a thriving nineteenth-century coal-mining community outside of San Francisco. Among other things, the experience gave us a new appreciation for the hard realities of life in that bygone era of the Old West.

As you explore the cemetery, notice the dates on the headstones and consider the brevity of human existence. Imagine what everyday life might have been like for those buried here, and consider the ways in which they might have made use of their time. Then consider the fact that you and everyone else now alive will probably be dead within the next hundred years.

Consider, also, which, if any, aspects of your own existence you

might consider somehow "eternal," and which may be fleeting illusions in the endless ebb and flow of space and time.

Complete today's session by taking some time to celebrate the
mundane joys of everyday existence. Go out for a pizza, take in a
movie, or visit a close friend.

DAY 30

THE TIMES OF YOUR LIFE

What if you knew you were going to die in six
months? Would you feel that yours had been a life well lived, full
of meaning, purpose, and fulfillment? Or would you wish you had
done something entirely different with your limited time on Earth?
How would you expect to be remembered, if you were remembered
at all? How would you like to spend the last six months of your life?

For the final exercise of the Higher Consciousness Program,
imagine that your life may turn out to be much shorter than you ever
expected. Find a private place to sit, away from the daily scene of
your everyday life, such as a hillside overlooking a beach or a rooftop
overlooking the skyline of a city.

Relax and ask yourself, "What is the most valuable, meaningful,
and worthwhile thing I can be doing with my life?" Is there some
long-postponed creative project that you've always hoped to carry
out "someday," if only you could somehow find the time? Is there
someplace you've always wanted to go, or something you've always
wanted to experience firsthand?

What would it take to begin pursuing your innermost dreams of
personal fulfillment and accomplishment right *now*? Focus on a single, small, easily carried-out action that would symbolically start
you on the path of fulfilling your fantasy today. If you've always
wanted to be a successful artist, for example, but never found the
time to learn to paint, you may decide to begin by buying an empty
canvas, or signing up for a painting course at your local art school
or college. If you've always fantasized about taking a trip to Tahiti,

you might decide to begin by stopping by a travel agent to pick up some brochures.

Whatever you decide, tell yourself that your dream is well within your grasp. Visualize yourself accomplishing the dream, and imagine how it will feel to achieve it. Then vow to set apart some time every day—or at least every week—to actively pursue your project in earnest. As you do so, keep in mind that you are taking direct responsibility for the course of your own life, and continue to imagine yourself getting closer and closer to fulfilling your wildest dreams.

> **Transcendental Tip**—By pursuing this final exercise on an active basis, you may achieve the highest sense of consciousness of all: the realization that the way in which you decide to live your life is a creative and fluid process, and that the seemingly ordinary world of mundane, ordinary existence may not really be that mundane or ordinary after all. You *can* experience a broad range of consciousness and fulfill a greater range of your personal potential—without abandoning your worldly existence.

In the meantime, continue to celebrate the mystical in everything you feel and see. After all, you should know how—you have just completed our 30-day course in Higher Consciousness. Good luck!

DAY 29
THE GRATEFUL
DEAD

DAY 30
THE TIMES
OF YOUR LIFE

Visit a cemetery with gravesites from many different historical eras.

Explore the cemetery, noticing the dates on the headstones. Consider the brevity of human existence.

Imagine what everyday life might have been like for those buried here, and consider the ways in which they might have made use of their time.

Consider the fact that you and everyone else now alive on the earth will probably be dead within the next hundred years.

Consider which, if any, aspects of your own existence you might consider somehow "eternal," and which may be fleeting illusions in the endless ebb and flow of space and time.

Celebrate the mundane joys of everyday existence. Go out for a pizza, take in a movie, or visit a close friend.

Find a private place far from the scenes of your everyday life. Imagine that your life may turn out to be much shorter than you ever expected.

Relax and ask yourself what you wish you were doing with your life.

Focus on a single act that would symbolically start you on the path toward fulfilling your fantasy today.

Tell yourself that your dream is well within your grasp. Visualize yourself accomplishing your goal, and imagine achieving it.

Vow to set apart some time every day —or at least every week— to actively pursue your project in earnest.

Continue to celebrate the mystical in everything you see and feel.

A SPECIAL NOTE TO THE
PHYSICALLY DISABLED

*F*or the sake of simplicity, the instructions for many of the exercises in the Higher Consciousness Program appear to assume certain basic physical capabilities. We sincerely hope, however, that the Higher Consciousness Program will attract a diverse readership, including many individuals who may have a wide variety of physical disabilities. In fact, there is absolutely no reason why the techniques presented in the Higher Consciousness Program cannot be practiced by everyone.

In much of our research at the Institute for Advanced Psychology, disabled individuals have made a significant contribution to our exploration and understanding of a wide range of extended human capabilities. We therefore request that our disabled readers bear with us, and that they feel free to adapt the various Higher Consciousness Program exercises to their personal capabilities and preferences.

We suggest, for example, that if you are blind, hearing impaired, confined to a wheelchair, or otherwise restricted in your ability to easily move around your environment, that you simply adjust the exercises to your particular needs; we assure you that the program will work just as well. We also remind you that many of the Higher Consciousness Program exercises are easily adaptable to a wide variety of available sensory and psychological approaches. If necessary, it is completely acceptable to skip a particular exercise, simply replacing it with another more suited to your requirements on a particular day. It is also always acceptable to proceed at a pace that feels most comfortable for you and works best in your individual situation.

We thank you for your interest and participation in the Higher Consciousness Program. We hope it will add a new dimension of enriching inner exploration and experience to your life.

Keith Harary and Pamela Weintraub

ACKNOWLEDGMENTS

We wish to express our sincere gratitude to our spouses: Mark Teich, who continues the quest, and Darlene Moore, the original everyday mystic.

We would also like to thank our colleagues and friends who have helped us explore the psychological and personal meaning of Mystical Experiences, especially those whose suggestions we have drawn upon in developing the Higher Consciousness Program. Our special appreciation to Earl Disselhorst, who suggested spending time in silence, Mary Catharine Farley, who recommended focusing on color, and Murray Cox and Greg Hooper for their invaluable suggestions.

Special thanks also go to our talented and supportive editor, Robert Weil, who came up with the 30-day concept, and Bill Thomas of St. Martin's Press, for his additional good-natured support. We would also like to express our sincere appreciation to our literary agents, Roslyn Targ and Wendy Lipkind.

Finally, our very special thanks to our insightful friend Patrice Adcroft, editor of *Omni* magazine, where variations on some of the Higher Consciousness Program exercises first appeared in December 1988. We would also like to acknowledge Kathy Keeton and Bob Guccione, whose vision of *Omni* inspired us to make Mystical Experiences accessible to the public.

We also extend our appreciation to the board of directors and board of scientific advisors of the Institute for Advanced Psychology for their role in furthering advanced psychological research.

ABOUT THE AUTHORS

Keith Harary, Ph.D., is internationally known for his pioneering contributions to scientific research on altered states of consciousness and extended human abilities. Dr. Harary, who holds a Ph.D. in psychology with emphases in both clinical counseling and experimental psychology, has authored and coauthored more than sixty popular and professional articles on topics relating to advanced psychological research and other areas. His work has been discussed in dozens of scientific and popular publications and more than two dozen books. He is also coauthor, with Pamela Weintraub, of *Have an Out-of-Body Experience in 30 Days: The Free Flight Program; Lucid Dreams in 30 Days: The Creative Sleep Program; Inner Sex in 30 Days: The Erotic Fulfillment Program*; and coauthor of the best-selling book, *The Mind Race*. He is President and Research Director of the Institute for Advanced Psychology in San Francisco.

Pamela Weintraub is editor at large at *Omni* magazine, where she has worked on staff for the past nine years. She was previously a staff writer at *Discover* magazine. Her numerous articles have appeared in *Omni, Penthouse, Discover, Health, Ms., Longevity*, and many other national publications. In addition to coauthoring the three books mentioned above with Keith Harary, she is author of *The Omni Book of Interviews*, and *Omni's Catalog of the Bizarre*.

FOR FURTHER INFORMATION ON HUMAN SEXUALITY RESEARCH AND GRADUATE STUDY OPPORTUNITIES

Institute for Advanced Study of Human Sexuality
1523 Franklin Street
San Francisco, California
94109

(not affiliated with the Institute for Advanced Psychology)

THE 30-DAY HIGHER CONSCIOUSNESS SERIES

Mystical Experiences in 30 Days is the fourth of an ongoing St. Martin's Press New Age 30-Day series. Also available through your bookstore or by writing St. Martin's Press are *Inner Sex in 30 Days: The Erotic Fulfillment Program*; *Have an Out-of-Body Experience in 30 Days: The Free Flight Program*; and *Lucid Dreams in 30 Days: The Creative Sleep Program*. All of these titles are written by Keith Harary, Ph.D., and Pamela Weintraub, and can be either specially ordered through your bookstore if currently not in stock, or directly ordered through St. Martin's Press by writing:
St. Martin's Press, Customer Service, 175 Fifth Avenue, New York, New York 10010.
New titles to complement this New Age series will be released in the coming months and subsequent years.
We would like to hear about your experiences with the Higher Consciousness Program for possible inclusion in a new book. Please contact us at:

The Institute for Advanced Psychology
Box 875
2269 Chestnut Street
San Francisco, CA 94123